Water Lines

New and Selected Poems

Luci Shaw

William B. Eerdmans Publishing Company
Grand Rapids, Michigan / Cambridge, U.K.

Wm. B. Eerdmans Publishing Co.
255 Jefferson Ave. S.E., Grand Rapids, Michigan 49503 /
P.O. Box 163, Cambridge CB3 9PU U.K.
www.eerdmans.com

Printed in the United States of America

08 07 06 05 04 03   7 6 5 4 3 2 1

Library of Congress Cataloging-in-Publication Data

Shaw, Luci
     Water Lines : new and selected poems / Luci Shaw.
        p. cm.
      ISBN 0-8028-2235-5 (alk. paper)
       1. Water — Poetry.   I. Title

     PS3569.H384W38 2003
     811'.54—dc21

                                        2003052855

Book design by James Thomas Chiampas

for Barbara Braver

contents

introduction

"Ahead . . . a leaf falls from high up in a long and gentle fall. In the water its reflection rises perfectly to meet it."

Wendell Berry

"You visit the earth and water it abundantly; the river of God is full of water. You drench the furrows and smooth out the ridges; with heavy rain you soften the ground and bless its increase."

Psalm 65:9-10, NIV

Water lines. Aqueducts and swimming pool lanes and lakes, water paths and pools, sluices and sources and vast stretches of water, the lines that drops of rain or snowflakes make as they fall in the air. And there are other *water lines* — of words on a page to form a poem. I've tried to pull the lines together here — a large, diverse, and radiant necessity. As an example of my love affair with water, this is what I wrote in my journal recently:

> I am lying on a single bed in the guest house of a college in Tennessee. I have been guest-lecturing much of the day. Exhausted and spiritually drained, I open the window so that I can be comforted by the fresh smell of the night as I lie under my warm bedclothes. I know that as I continue my series of

daily chapel messages on spiritual renewal, I need personal replenishing. I welcome the silky river of cool air as it breathes across my face, reminding me of the breath of God, which can refresh my tired soul. Through the window I can actually *hear* leaves falling with a brittle, golden rustle, the way cornflakes are supposed to sound, if we believe the commercials.

Beech leaves. I've been seeing them all day as I've walked around campus. They are curled and crisp enough to make an audible impact as they land on other recently fallen beech leaves, bright brown like the color of a bay horse's rump, not dull, but varnished and glowing, a layered nation of dry leaves.

Then the click sounds of falling come more frequently, a patter with a sense of splash. I realize it is raining.

The steady hush of falling rain, the white noise of a waterfall, the glittering sounds of a fountain, the washing of ripples against rocks in a clear northern lake, of a surging mountain stream — all of them refresh the ear and the eye, and from there they penetrate the soul. The sea has its own effect on me — its endless series of breakers thundering in, sending arcs of foaming lace up the tilting sands to my feet, then drawing back with its silver foil. I think it's the fluidity of water — the way it constantly renews itself — that reminds me of the possibility, and the need, for change and renewal.

Another thing. I love water's imperturbability, its persistence. It may surge, roar, pour, pool, spring, sprinkle, splash, weep, trickle, refresh, gurgle, ripple, drip, freeze, crystallize, avalanche or evaporate, irrigate or flood, but it never ceases to be. It continues to cycle through our existence, subtle or bold, masking itself or showing off. Though it is caught in the trap of atmosphere, within that restriction it moves freely and ceaselessly across the globe and through our lives.

I used to live in dry California, commuting, often by car, to the state of Washington and the province of British Columbia, where rain arrives in weather fronts that wash like waves across the northern reaches of the continent, and where mist and fog deposit their gift of moisture, making all the gardening enthusiasts (and the gardens) happy. Driving north through the mountains of northern California and Oregon, gradually entering this aqueous zone, I felt my spirit being rehydrated after the dryness.

When we live in one of the arid areas of our continent, what strenuous efforts we make to discover new sources of water! In states like Arizona and Nevada and New Mexico, immense sums of money — and endless effort — are spent developing systems that will deliver fast-dwindling supplies of water by canal, by underground pipes, even by low-flying planes, to maintain water-thirsty crops, parks, lawns. From our omniscient airborne viewpoint, we're familiar with those green circles of growth that we spot in a valley otherwise completely pallid, dry, and barren. Someone has either piped water up from an aquifer or diverted it from a remote river, and the transformation of the landscape is immediate and visible. Water is, quite simply, the essential element for life: without it we would dry up and die.

Unless we have lived in the desert, we may not be aware of the vivid contrast between dryness, the result of drought, and greenness, the consequence of irrigation. It became strikingly apparent to me during a visit to Israel. With a carload of friends I drove down from Jerusalem into the arid valley through which the Jordan River flows into the salty Dead Sea. We dropped fourteen hundred feet as we followed the winding road from the Mount of Olives to Dead Sea level. The deeper we plunged, the higher the temperature rose, until at 10 A.M. it had reached 115 degrees, and we commented that our skin felt dehydrated enough to crack. When we reached the bottom of the valley, there, before us, in its setting of a vast, barren landscape of glare and heat, gleamed the green jewel that is Jericho.

Just inside the town limits we stopped at a roadside fruit stall where baskets of loquats and kumquats, oranges and figs, sacks of almonds, tubs of olives, and jars of honey awaited our shekels. There was a striking contrast between the side of the street on our left — which stretched, a dusty wilderness, bare and lifeless, all the way to the glittering Salt Sea — and the Jericho side of the street, verdant with palm trees, citrus groves, enormous, shady fig trees, and myriad luxuriant flowering vines and shrubs. "So this is what *an oasis* means," I thought. "It means fruitfulness and health where all around it is sterility and death."

Jericho's secret? If I stood quite still and listened, I could hear the gurgle of water running through the stone-lined irrigation channels, aqueducts open to the sky, crisscrossing the town in every direction, pulsing with clear water rising from underground springs, making it possible for the residents to grow not only large trees but vineyards and acres of vegetables. *Water is the secret of life.* Where the aqueducts ended, the desert began again. Standing in the cool shade, I could see how water had made possible the kind of verdure described in Isaiah 58:11: "The LORD . . . will satisfy your needs in a sun-scorched land. . . . You will be like a well-watered garden, like a spring whose waters never fail."

We can learn a lot about the land by observing the growth it produces, and the way it holds water. Driving in the countryside of New Zealand's South Island, from a distance I could guess at the presence of a stream, or even the damp seepage from an underground spring, simply by noticing the twisting line of willows that followed the waterline, hugging its contours, curving along the creases between the folds and flanks of the hillsides. And it's not too difficult to notice the traces of green in a fruitful life that has been watered by the hidden springs of the Spirit.

We all need water at our roots. As the poet G. M. Hopkins cried, "O thou Lord of my life, send my roots rain!" Often it's our own tears that water our hearts most deeply and beneficially. Tears spring up and fill our eyes and spill down our cheeks for many reasons. Though there can be tears of joy and relief — a lost child found, a marriage restored, a long wait rewarded — as in "weeping may endure for a night, but joy comes in the morning" — most tears have to do with pain, sorrow, loss, grief, or remorse. Besides being a release and a relief when we are burdened or troubled beyond endurance, they are also an evidence that our hearts are tender, touchable, and teachable. Just as a field in early spring is moistened by the weeping of melting snow, allowing that field to be cultivated and receptive to the seed, so our souls may be watered by our tears. *Non sine sole iris,* which means "no rainbow without the sun"; *non sine lacrimae iris* — no rainbow without the rain of tears, either.

Water was probably the first mirror, long before glass had been manufactured, before people gazed in fascination at their faces reflected back from highly polished brass or bronze surfaces. Of course, we see our undistorted image only in a reflection from still water. Perhaps if we had stillness deep within us, we might view the world, and ourselves, with truer perception. How do we attain this stillness? It's a question that I need to ask myself often, pulled as I am in a thousand directions by other people's urgencies and by my own desire to accomplish things — or, if I am honest with myself, to satisfy my own longing for significance.

On a recent afternoon I went down our front garden path to our roadside mailbox to leave a letter for the mailman. I could see the mail truck up the road, and I was anticipating a couple of important letters, so I waited out there for him to come. I was impatient, having several tasks to complete before dinner, but suddenly I was struck by the thought, "This is a chance to be still, to savor the moment." And so I waited, standing on our brick garden path, smelling the woodsy smell of the wet, fallen oak leaves, and listening as a squirrel fidgeted noisily in the tree above me. The moss between the bricks was emerald velvet. The sky was lit with lemon-colored clouds. And I was content, glad to be quiet and let my soul be at rest, undistracted by the slowness of the mailman's measured progress from mailbox to mailbox. For our souls' health, we need to take — or make — these moments of stillness, when we can let the world of nature, and of nature's Creator, speak to us in our interior world. Refreshment. *Re-freshment.*

And still waters run deep, as the old proverb has it. I ask myself, Would I rather be a wide, shallow, meandering river, or one that is narrowly channeled between its banks, cutting deeply, over the ages, into its streambed by reason of its strong current? If I'm honest, I guess I'd like to be both wide *and* deep. Like an ocean, maybe?

Water evokes in us emotional responses as diverse as gratitude, bliss, excitement, serenity, and refreshment. Water is also capable of appealing to our senses, attuned as they are to natural phenomena. Consider the sibilance of water, its sensuousness, how it cries out to be tasted, felt, smelled, heard, seen, experienced, enjoyed. Explore with me some of the facets of water in this book of poems that arose, one by one, out of a life touched by water, pooling as it has in the Creator's hand and falling, like blessing, on all our heads.

Luci Shaw
Bellingham, Washington

Between the lines

I can't help noticing
how falling leaves and rain
print their trajectories —
traces in the air, on the window glass —
as if writing some cosmic equation.

My algebra was always bad but
trigonometry — its angles
and curves, its tangents and sines
and signs — always wakes something
quite beyond logic in my heart.

As if the mystery of existence were becoming
visible — my small gasps of prayer,
meant to rise, not fall, triangulating
in the wind. And the simple
snow — each flake unique, intact, as it

flies through space — giving chaos
a chance to re-integrate to a kind of holy
order, filling cracks, hollows — the muddy ruts
in the playing field behind the school
white, beautifully level again.

Below

Water bottom, stones cold and
sharp to my naked heel
under the dappled slur and waver
of what salmon know as air — wind
through angled mouth and out gills —
a magnification of colored gravel,
a blurred glaze, a limpid drift,
in winter a sleeve of ice.

What I'm trying for is this: low down
the river's skin — its wrestle and repose,
its purl and ripple — answers back to
the light behind the float of clouds,
the invisible galaxies tenting the air.
Under the transient sheet of atmosphere
yellow leaves fly the currents until
they are caught, blazing, under
the lens of water, or rot to humus;
banks erode; sediment builds; pebbles
disintegrate as gravity drags.

Yet with all this force, this wheel
and whirl, how buoyant the water striders.
How the high meadows itch

with green. And the itinerant red-tail hawk —
how freely he cruises the halls of air.
How well the silver fish hold their own
in the current, heads to the source.
How easily the dragonfly nymphs sideslip
along the riffle, up to their ears in light.

Camping in
the Rockies

After four days in the mountains
we have lived most of the world's
history — its passionate storms,
its silences of fog, the exuberant valleys
and ruinous cliffs, and above
the timberline its tundra of small,
pink flowers shivering on short wires,
that remind me of me, quivering
in the kiss of your breath.

Our uncertainty reveals itself
the way a mountain campanula
half-opens its purple mouth — waxy,
mysterious, tracked by a black thread
of ants. If I could be as sure about us
as the politicians seem to be about campaign
promises. . . . The truth is, the future lies
in ambush; more waits to happen

like the surprise of thunder
when Glacier Lake, blue as a peacock
feather, carrying God's gold solar eye,
turns black with wind.

Against entropy

Consider our perception of glaciers —
the shoulders of mountains scaffolded with ice
as if their age-old bulk might collapse under
its own weight, needs shoring up.
Or the shape-shift of rain to crystals,
gravity settling the grainy flakes, the wind picking up,
wrapping the houses with false comfort —
a fleeced scarf that grows to a drift. As if
the world, in its bleakest season,
craves warmth, is reaching for refuge. Ponder

the limbs of fir trees with their sloping
shelves of white about to fall, the rib cage
around the singing lungs not
giving in; the brittle bones still upholding
the ripening body like crutches
against collapse. Even a minimal movement,
like closing the window against the draught,
or lighting a small fire, reverses
entropy, thaws the iron authority
of the season. Tomorrow, when sunlight hits,
the frost will steam up from our sidewalks,
the black ice will melt on the pass.

Inside outside

Inside the house, all
you see are the streams of rain
down the windows. Outside,
even a minute exposes you to
the chill splash of truth as the singular drops
filter through your dark hair
and trickle down your scalp,
soaking the collar at your neckline.
Shivering, you intuit the needle of ice
that still lives like a seed
at the heart of each drop — it feels that cold.

Would you wish yourself innocent
of ice, shielded? This is a poem
you could never have written, a frost
you would never have let yourself feel.

Raining

Like spun silk, water strives
to find its end, a fluid form.
It shapes itself to multitudes of leaves
and riverbeds, and overhanging eaves.

Gravity pulls the silver down,
a fluid tent around the porch,
with filaments like fishing lines. Thin ropes
of crystal beads (their shining drops

each singing its own syncopated sound
into the pail we set to catch the drips)
have raised the level so the pitch
climbs higher every hour, in the round

tin bucket, till it's full up to the brim.
Like rain or sorrow, loving takes its time
to name its music
or to find a rhyme.

Freezing rain

Most of the things a poet has to say
are tentative, lists of foggy clues
and suppositions — an unattested version
of the way the wind breathes at night,
an essay at atmosphere, predictions
as unreliable as weather forecasts. I stab
at the truth with a pencil sometimes,
moved too suddenly to words by
the shadings on a cloud, or its shape,
shivering at a hint of thunder (sure
that it means something).

But in the lines set down on paper
all suggestions become categorical —
intuition or illusion edited to sound
like logic. Naked ideas turn assertive
in print, sharp, as intricate as the edges
of a woods in winter seen against
a black sky. The most fluid
of impressions hardens like frozen rain.
A cold front is passing over: I hazard
a guess; you take it for reality.

Great Blue Heron

　　From the corner of
one eye I see the ungainliness
dropping its stilt legs past my window
onto the lily pond's edge.
In the fan of water that lifts
and lowers, lifts and lowers
across the grass, wing feathers
fold from the shape of flight
into a blue umbrella — almost purple
against the green.

　　To see a heron is
a good omen, I was told once
after I had watched a visitation.
Like gray praying prophets, heralds
of something Other, they had
elbowed their way down to
the creek that threads itself past my
wild cabin, north by at least
a thousand miles.

　　What does it mean to see
an omen for good? Just this:
Because I love that far valley of rain

I've wanted to believe good. Now,
in the haunting of this holy
stalker of water, this picker of fish,
its odd body contoured in the sprinkler,
I follow a blue thread of promise
pulled south.

North St. Vrain Creek, Colorado

". . . the creek rests the eye, a haven, a breast."

Annie Dillard

Between fringed banks she mounds, breasting
over water-bottom, shadow-nippled, naked, skinned
with sky and aspen leaves and dragonflies,
bellying between the shining boulder, a fluid
flesh but firm with the force of her going.
From the bridge at noon the heat of his seeing
knuckles down at her, senses jump the gap,
his eyes drink until the cool pools in his brain,
soaks down the thirsty length of him. As she
has found an interval's home in his eye, he
has discovered haven from the day's blaze
in her body of water.

Vacation video

As we drive East, the landscape
develops like a film: seamless prairies
give way to a chronicle of forests
spliced with plots of hops and potatoes.
The horizon exposes itself in a suspense
of green crests. Incidental rivers
and other bodies of water unroll and join
in one — vast, salt, smelling of fish.

Two weeks later, the trip home from
the shore runs the whole vacation backwards:
lobster pots vanish, sand falls from our
shoes, a lost beach towel reappears like
a special effect, the scenery relaxes
into flatness. What if our lives could be
re-run? Our journey taken over?

Orienting

This night is multi-leveled.
I feel sliced in layers, walking
the beach path at night. Scattered high —
broken glass on an infinite black parking lot —
the sharp stars glitter. Lower down
the tops of trees, dark and
undifferentiated, boil like a line
of low clouds. And there,
between the trees, the horizon's
silver edge bisects heaven from earth.

Around me at chest level fog
settles in strips thick as bandages,
drifting between me and my feet
so that every step I take hides
from me. I am divided, myself
from myself, like one of Escher's
spiral people unfurling in a ribbon.
I peer through aqueous air
shivering with paradox: seeing
so far, hesitating so near.

But this is a universe that grinds
at glib appearances. Gravity

pulls at me relentlessly through
my soles. Infinity beckons. And when
a wedge of air, silent as Spirit,
like a knife from Long Island Sound,
cuts across the marshes, it peels back
the cataract of fog almost surgically.
Gauze rolls off in layers until
I am joined again, moving ahead,
foot by foot, navigating both by stars
and the stones on the path.

Mixed media

Finned, masked, body bright as a bone
under water, traced with tricks of waves' edges,
I have left land to shift into new gear. It is
like flying — weightless, floating. Thighs
slick as a seal's sides, I fluke through
colored schools of scales that turn at a flick,
glint past my foreign cheek. Or I can hang
motionless in the caves of light, clear as air.
My hands, down-branched like sea-stalks,
touch at a coral's rasp, and the pink weeds'
slip and frill.

    Having swum like a gull, I long now
to crease the sea's skin, to break water,
to rise airborne, to fly, gliding easy as a fish,
to clothe bird bones, wings angled
flat as planes, plucked high, dripping,
by the lift of feathers, the balance of beak
and body, the up-trusting eye — Oh,
to be at home in the sea, and as clean
and careless, there in the fathomless sky!

Edges of Wales

Stalking the blind lanes, striding to the hill
top before daybreak, often I've ached at the sweet chill
of spring light glittering through an intricacy
of leaves, when, in its precision of green, every tree
turns candle. With a series of airy, sharp surprises
crow's wings fold pearly heaven. Then the full sun rises,
polishing the view — stones quick and wet as steel,
glitter on a cobweb, gravel under my heel.

But on this early day in May, I wake
through light opaque as milk. The hedgerows make
mysteries with the mist. The cries of sheep shiver
the drenched air. Like silk sliding away, the river
moves south, the sheen of its crease
supple between banks and bushes blanched as fleece.
I thought I loved the hard, bright edges best
until I melted in this morning's mist.

Trace

Because you walk
on water
your footprints
are invisible.

Yet we keep looking
for a wet mark
from the ball
of your foot
or even
a lick of
dried salt
on the stones.

Look!

As we learned how to read,
were we beginning to forget to look,
our young eyes caught in tangles of print
so that imagination was choked? Were we
trapped at that remove from ourselves?

Or did we begin to see a new way, with eyes
that widened in the amazement of reverie,
memory, invention? As we peered
between the words, could we make out
shapes and colors beyond them?

What did our inside eyes make of
the black marks on creamy paper, on onionskin?
A dream of angels turned real, perhaps.
A wooden boat on a lake. Three small loaves
fragmented to fill all those empty mouths

and baskets. Or this: a blind man
opening his eyes so that the first face he sees —
a vision, surely — is Christ's, spittle
still shining on the quick fingers,
his mouth saying urgently, Look!

Negligible

The ant, brief as a second,
lone scout of dew and peony petals,
black on cream. Easy to pluck,
and a trifling crunch
under foot.

The dust mite also,
invisible to the eye, invading
pillows, mattresses, with her
generations — fuse for my
explosive allergies.

Assumed: that we will stand in awe
of larger things, like the bulldozer
tearing the ancient cedars
from the lot down the road. Or a bomb.
Or the oceans. Or the expanding universe.

But let us up-end our thoughts:
What matchstick of vexation
lights the slow wick of rancor.
How like a parasite
it eats at our gut.

And how one moment's
catalytic radiance (think St. Clare,
at Portiuncula) tilts, overturns the universe,
plants our feet on heaven's
widening threshold.

Bee

An image hurtles against the glass,
frantic to get out into a world of three
or more dimensions. Like being suddenly
transfigured, a collision with sunlight.
The surprise, the shock of heat, the colors,
bright as silk. The rush of nectar.

Anguish or bliss? Or both at once?
Intensity doubles the shift,
translates it brilliant enough
to expose its allegory on the brain's film,
the shoe-box memory
where prints are stored, secure even after
cataracts and a smashed camera.

Fall, and raining, but summer
glows from the garden still,
the shriveled lilies like grave-clothes.
The bee, distilling honey from the hearts
of old flowers, its body a coal
burning with pollen.

Striders

Frio River, Laity Lodge, Texas

This is what happened. The junipers
on the bank blue with berries. The hot sun.
The limestone river running shallow as spring.
The thin beige water boiling a radiant six-inch arc —
the mystery. A freshet breathing up from underground?
An errant current? A pentecostal riffle of air?

We were there, transfixed by
the knot of intensity on the water's skin — a commotion
of insects, gray-brown, each less than a fly, the visual buzz
of their hysteria a fury of desire, an orgasm of arthropods,
a script for survival, a narrative of miniature flesh
brainstorming the next generation.

Silk

She is an amber eye framed
by the black lashes of her legs.

Poet of the chasm, she draws
from her own belly a tensile strand

that links things — trellis to mailbox,
leaf to leaf — and spreads a hammock

for the diamond rain. She erects
a scaffold for the fragilities

of twiggy birches, one part steel
to ten of air; like mercy, or hunger,

it is new every morning.
It is her strategy to weave

invisibility. Careless, any one of you
can sweep her star out of the sky

with your elbow. But needing
a lesson in patience, you could stay

and watch her architecture's diligent
re-creation. Art complete,

she swings free at tether's end,
explorer, parachutist, mountaineer

rappelling space. Then, born for devouring
and begetting, she centers herself,

head down, pregnant heart
of the snare, to wait for the silly gnats.

The amphibian

Warm
after a while on a rock,
drunk with sky, her green silk
shrivels with wind. With a wet,
singular sound, then, she creases
the silver film, turns fluid,
her webbed toes accomplishing
the dark dive to water bottom and
the long soak, until her lungs,
spun for air, urge her up
for breath.

She moves
in two worlds, caught between
upper and under, never home.
Restless — skin withering for wet,
and the nether ooze,
or nostrils aching to fill
with free air her bubble lungs,
heart thumping, tympanum
throat pulsing to flood
the deepening sky with loud
frog song.

Seeing the Shore

At ebb tide the sands are stretched —
flat, damp, written on with rain, woven
with a warm air from the west.
As the tide moves in again,
each succeeding wave spells
a new boundary in a sweeping sentence
punctuated with foam. Its drawing back
pulls a silver foil across the slope.
The film flows, thins, clouds
like a breath-touched mirror, sinks
into the body of the shore.

Your marriage is a beach — a spread of
weeds and wet edges and shells
(pink-lipped, unanchored seeds from
the sea floor, left in the open air
and high tide, like love-notes).
Now let the seasons shift your singing
sands, let the wind lift and level you,
let water — salt, or fresh from the sky —
shape all the grainy contours
of your joining into ribs and rivulets
and pools for snails and

sea anemones. Let the roar and roll
of breakers polish the quartz and agate
in your detritus. Like gulls, move
with the moment. Have no fear; the edges
of the earth, the rims of rock are a
foundation under you. You will not
be swept out to sea.

Beach, Aberystwyth, Wales

Without expecting anything extraordinary
we were, as always, magnetized
by the idea of sea, drawn down the stone steps
    to the shingle,
with the blue-black sky glooming behind,
    light-washed pastel verticals on our left —
the beach hotels. We turned away from
    the morning glare,
crunched along the shoal into
the stretched shadow of the broken castle,
dodged the scatter of debris left by
the Bank Holiday crowds, and crossed
a barrier of rocks. Then, as if our ears
suddenly came open, the sea's huge sound
hit — waves pounding forward into thunder,
    then sucking back and away

through what sounded like skeletons — a bruising
    grind and rattle,
racket and clutch as though a cobble of vertebrae
    had been thrown up by
the Irish Sea. This boneyard hummed up through

our soles. Our ears rang
　　with the songs of fierce minimal stones. Mussel shells
　　　　lay about, sprung open like pillboxes,
　　stinging the view (such livid blue inside the dull
　　　　black casings). And the small surprises
of sea glass, eyes clipped from once-useful green
　　　　and cobalt bottles, the colors
of oceans condensed, rubbed by marine restlessness
　　　　to fragments soft and blind

as sea-breath. Crab carapaces gone limp,
　　　　no longer crisp with life. The sea itself sliced
by knives of wind, latticed like fish scales,
　　　　hiding beneath its netted frown
a glimmer of pearls and shells, and jellies
　　　　floating deep like perfect, archetypal
parachutes of light — invisible to us, but we knew
　　　　they were there. And we,
since Eden we have been wanderers, all of us,
　　　　blasted with wind-driven sand,
sometimes scattered wide like driftwood, like
　　　　the great leg bones of sea monsters,

sometimes a mere flash of rinded color, left
　　　on the shore with the stranded rose-red
kelp bladders, the plastic cups, the soaked beach rags
　　　of the careless. We need reminding
of what we were meant to be before we reached
　　　too far, too fast, and were forced
to feel the chop of the fire blade, the despairing bubble
　　　of flood, the wrack, the ruin. This is what
we have become: flesh, splendid, weak, and brief;
　　　only our bones and souls persist.

Just before noon the moment's fair weather
　　　drained away like a spirit rising, the color
wiped from the faces of the hotels,
　　　the dark castle crumbling grain by grain.

Evaporation

Thirty years ago the green square beyond
our back door was webbed with lines
on which I hung with wooden pegs
my angels and my ghosts — white nightgowns
winged in the wind, shrouds of tablecloths,
shirts fluting their spooky sleeves, their
dwindling tails — shadows of the lucid cloth
moving like water on the grass.

Now we live over a basement dryer churning
beneath a 40-watt bulb. The trap keeps filling
with a gray lint as our clothes, our second skins,
are dried out by the minutes on a dial.
The air behind the house
is empty of epiphanies, apparitions.
Gone is the iron-fresh smell of damp linens
praying their vapor to the sun.

Birthright

Inherited from my father: a set of genes
that, right from the start, exhibited passion,
recklessness, a disdain for caution,
a debonair rashness, a willingness
to jump off any diving platform
though the water below was chunked
with ice floes. An aversion to enclosures.
Spiritual fervor, too, a roaring flame
in him (and in me, somewhere
deep, a glowing coal waiting for wind).

From my mother, bearing me, her first,
at forty-six, anxiety and an avid ownership
(to enhance her own sense of self?),
a need to keep hazard at bay.
Mating in me, their roil of genetic oil
and water still sings its iridescent storm,
its contrasts between my tide's ebbs and flows,
its weather fronts, the highs and lows that
yield a brilliant heat, a chilling snow.

Labor

After her daughter's wedding
she cleaned out the bedroom — rolling up
the posters of Venice, the Greek
islands, virginal sails like wings
in golden bays. Surveying the naked
closet and walls from the doorway
she felt the chill, as though she had
just expelled her afterbirth. And from

some deep place she remembered —
that beginning of loss, a pushing out
and out that left the matrix hollow,
the newborn's muted cry still
echoing, another expulsion, another
wave good-bye. Every division of cells
widens the change. The ripples circle out,
the boat leaves harbor.

Sailing
San Francisco Bay

She braces — one hand
on the forestay. Her other hand
curves around to the outside of the jib,
its belly heavy with wind.

Pressing against her hand-heel,
deceptive as silk, the air
fills the sail cloth until it bulks
as pregnant as her own body
before each birth. Out there
on the Catalina's prow, with
the small waves swelling against
the hull under her so that
through the soles of her deck shoes
she feels the waters breaking,
she is alone, letting it all go
with the water sliding away below.
The other sounds — curlew cries across
the water, Mozart on the portable player,
the glasses and voices from the cabin —
all trail behind, like the faint call of her
grown children, gone in the green wake.

It is all such old magic — bittersweet
like birth, the melting sea silver
stained sky red, vanishing between
her legs like the last light being sucked
down through the bones of the mountains,
there, in a bloody show.

She flattens her hand and pushes hard
against the blue cloth so that the sail
spills some of its wind,
giving it back to the bay.

Beach at Orient

Just now, I wish for someone
like me, for whom this stony beach
will be rinsed back suddenly
into something pure, for whom
these breakers will flatten themselves,
obeisant, at your feet, wetting each pebble
into its particular self.

Just now, as you and I begin
to walk the edge, I want for you
the companion eye, a hand, reaching
like mine for moonstones, agates,
translucencies in apricot, onyx, amber,
milk-white, each water-true. Your glance
singles out a winking bead of aqua
sea glass. Call it a mermaid's tear.
Call it an eye: it looks back.

And when, from the cold lip
of a wave, your fingers rescue a marble
of quartzite from a million others
and place it on my palm, burning
with its own light, just now
I witness a wish turning true.

Upon arrival from
the West Coast to be
with friends

From the *USA Today* weather map I know that
rain is falling on the open sea, far out.

The ocean is empty. There is no one to observe
the dark rug of rain that flattens waves,

the roiled surface pricked by drops that
celebrate their arrival from the heights

with such exuberant pirouettes, and a sound like
hands clapping (though no one hears).

What seems so crucial about these small particles
entering their great Mother, like birds home to the nest?

Whether or not we notice, water has always
welcomed its own into the bosom. As you with me.

Postcard from the shore

In a wide cloud, suddenly,
a thousand gulls lift
off the salt lagoon
into a corona
around the sun.

They circle
the slopes of air together,
moving so easily, cleanly,
my sand-clogged ankles
ache to run.

I am trying, now,
to tell you what it was like,
but words can only hint
at the moment of heart's dance,
the wonder of wings,
the folly of flight.

You would have had
to be with me, our heads
thrown back, our eyes full

of flashing feathers, our
eardrums pierced
with splinters of gull sound,
with audible light.

Resurrection:
Rocky York Islet, B.C.

Trial, error, and my blue kayak
have found me this rock shelf, curved
to fit my thighs, sun-warm as my blood.
Around me fractured coral-pink
crab carapaces and glistening scabs
of fish scales patch the water-weathered
sandstone; I realize
the resting place I've chosen is where
sea otters relieve themselves.

Waves lap, air breathes, and yet
there's not enough bird or beast in me
for permanent contentment on a
barren shoal. But in this moment
quiet falls like wisdom; glitter
unfurls in my eye; words swim onto
the notebook page to deposit their
small scat in phrases colored like
the indigestible scales of rainbow fish —
God raising what is dead to life.

Lament for a poet
just dead

When at last she died, all they could moan in grief was
Mother, mother. As though that was all she was to them,
as though all she'd accomplished her whole life
was maternity, as though all her conceptions had been

physical. Small memory of the lines of
glistening words like laundry hung to dry in the sun.
Or the envelopes of poems in mailboxes bursting
like spores into print. The weather balloons of

images rising, flying, their colored silk collapsing
on foreign beaches. Tell them: Try to remember
the gale of her passion like wind grating itself
against the corner of the beach house,

its wreath of fog streaming now, inescapable.
Tell them: Compass yourselves with its salty breath
and the whisper of foam and wrack and detritus
that still rises from the shore of her life.

Under the snowing

Under the snowing
the leaves lie still.
Brown animals sleep
through the storm, unknowing,
behind the bank and the frozen hill.
And just as deep
in the coated stream
the slow fish grope
through their own dark, stagnant dream.

Who on earth would hope
for a new beginning
when the crusted snow
and the ice start thinning?
Who would even know
that the night could stir
with warmth and wakening
coming, creeping,
for sodden root and fin and fur
and other things lonely
and cold and sleeping?

Spring, St. Martin's Chapel Cathedral of St. John the Divine

for Madeleine L'Engle

Both of us kneel, then wait
on the church chairs — square, chocolate brown —
knowing that soon the black priest

will hurry in, wearing his lateness like
the wrong robe. In the pregnant emptiness
before communion, that crack between worlds,

we listen inward, feet tight on the cold slate,
wanting to hear Christ tell us Feed on me.
Our hearts shiver, hidden. Nothing visible moves.

Outside a drizzle starts; drops spit on the sill.
The window bird flies motionless in
a cobalt sky of skillful glass.

But beyond the frame, plucking the eye
like a message from Outside, a minor shadow
tilts and swoops in light rain,

wings telling us to fly wide, loose
and nervy as sparrows who may peck crumbs from
any picnic table, or gnats right out of the air.

Fraction

Like the winter morning ice
that, brittle, skins a puddle —

like the wafer the priest lifts and snaps
with the fingers of his two hands —

a pistol shot across the congregation —
so is the name of Jesus splintered

to fall in fragments from our tongues,
sharpening the oath-speech

of the careless, feeding others
with light from the broken crystal.

The Golden Ratio &
the Coriolis Force*

This morning God himself — his wafer —
lay for a moment naked on my tongue.
I felt the blood of God race through my veins.
Week by week Christ's flesh gets
broken down in my own body cells, as
the platelets in my plasma, like an uncurling
swirl of skyward birds, like my life spiral,
maintain their slow unwinding.

The second law.

The hurricanes, like commas
on the weather map. Amoebas.
Waterspouts. Curled fetuses.
Convolvulus vines twisting anti-clockwise
on the trellis. Dust devils dancing over fields.
The spiral nebulae. The nautilus.
The human ear. The bathtub water
scrolling down the drain — everything
made by God looks God-like,
and these unfolding spirals seem to me
the shape of God. The universe, once

wound up, is now rewinding, like my life —
to zero and the Everything of God
(who lay this morning naked
on the manger of my tongue).

* The Coriolis force describes how moving objects, such as
  water going down a drain, are deflected as a result of the
  earth's rotation, spiraling right in the northern hemisphere
  and left in the southern hemisphere.

Holy Ghost

At the conference the cosmologists trade theories.
Attempting to nail down the how of Intelligent Design,
they scratch formulas on chalkboards and establish
the certain degrees of their uncertainty. Rational language
proves too meager for you, transcendent.

Flying home, bemused, through rafts of clouds,
I watch a rag of mist drift past the plane window.
Are you that — a wraith? Invisibility feeds my agnosticism,
yet an answer seems to come out of the blue:
"Even if you don't believe in ghosts, believe in me."

My imagination has always been a window for you
to open. Sometimes it's like this: a drab day, and then
a little dance begins in the brain — bubbles rising like yeast,
a quickening spirit hovering over the waters. Dreams begin
to come in three or more dimensions, rhythms pulse in waves,

phrases nudge me like little fists, sounds begin to click
together, green turns real enough to be written as a word
on paper. Skeptic, and no scientist, I am being tuned to
the narrative of heaven. My own poems persuade me the way
an available womb, and labor, persuade a baby to be born.

Prayer of the
holy hermit Basilea

Oh, my Lord, I pray that you will
love me with all your heart, as if I were
the only one.

That you will noose my vitals
with your thong so that your desire
becomes mine.

That you will strip me to the bone,
even to the joints clotted with pain, if that is
what it takes.

That your fierce, deliberate light
will bury itself in my brain until my eyes
are opened.

That you ignite Ezekiel in my mind,
so that his unearthly visions become
my habitation.

Matins, lauds, prime, terce, sext, nones, vespers,
compline — that your hours will pierce me with arrows
and wounds of praise.

That you inscribe your own urgent passion on
my flesh — your branded signature, until the smoke
goes up like incense.

That you salt my throat with thirst so ardent
that I am parched (one sip from your well of love
would sizzle),

then, dry as a week-old crust,
I pray you — consume me so that my wheat
becomes your fire.

That you suspend me, as you were, nailed
between upper and under, when neither will have me,
until both.

Bluff Edge,
Whidbey Island

This is the rock-rim edge of the known world.
This is the ragged planet where Christ landed,
and we are his people, craggy and knotted and burled,
and aching and lonely. Restless. Stranded.

These firs could well have framed his wooden manger
and his cross; I never encounter Advent without
Dark Friday. The days in the life of this stranger
were flecked with God-graces, threaded with human doubt.

Battered by storms of loss in her loving and grieving,
all her life Mary lived on the cliff-edge of cruel foresight.
Clinging, she rode the gusts and the glory, heaving
still with the donkey rhythm, dazzled with western light.

Slow Passage —
Teel's Island*

Though now you ride the crest of the field
and rise to the seasonal slow heaving
of the earth, the gulls are the same,
and the restless sky. Strong airs under you
still push the waves — salt grasses lifting darkly
to break in milkweed, yarrow, Queen Anne's lace.

Never, now, dolphins. Moles are the travelers
in your deeps. Field mice and crickets
dart among the weedy shallows at your stern.
Lichens barnacle your beam.
Only the rains wet your gray, shrunken wood.
Only wind slaps your sides. The far barn's
lightning rod is the lone compass needle
to tell you your true north. And oars I cannot see
pull, twist, and feather in your stiff rowlocks
to keep you heading west.

*Teel's Island *is the title of an Andrew Wyeth painting*
that shows an old dinghy stranded high in a field.

Leaving it all behind

Wye Valley, Wales, July 2002

From the cottage window the sweep
of wheat comforts and fills the eye.

The green glass of the river clears the mind,
drowns last week's urgencies.

Though I hear the harsh complaints
of a ewe from two hedgerows away

her sheeply concerns are not mine,
distanced from me by pastures,

honeysuckle, and a spread of purple
vetch. A bird is saying: Sweet. Sweet.

From an acre white with the lace of coriander
rises the steady murmur of bees. The breathy air

taps in my ear at intervals. It smells of hay,
blows a white moth, like a little silk rag,

into the next field. A mourning dove
proclaims peace: To you. To you, too.

Hills doze along the horizon, imperturbable.
The wasp of a motorcycle moves off

down the valley, leaving a stillness
that owes nothing to wind or lack of it,

as though the landscape itself
were practicing contemplation.

Puzzle: Tuolumne River

Just now, a yellow leaf the shape of an eye
flying, settling on glacial rock, watching us;

the river, spilling its slow snow-melt, conserving
its ancient secrets, its questions;

each hour a new riddle showing: the way water,
in its softness, knuckles holes in granite;

the sun's burn across ripples, crowding
the chill olive of shadow; the wedlock

of moss with pine root; your cascade's
cursive eloquence that drowns my mineral hush.

Camping

For Karen Cooper

The river rushes along in a hurry
to get somewhere. Our tent is pitched close;
above the oxymoron of its noisy hush
we, in folding chairs on the bank, wait
to slow down, to let the mind wander,
to turn primitive. Simplicity
is what we say we want — the current's
single-mindedness, even its monotony.

A week goes by. It would be so good
to be aimless. To be content to be aimless.

But we are mothers, keepers of homes.
At the campsite we work to keep the firewood dry,
the butter cool, the food secure from bears,
the tent zipped against mosquitoes,
the water heating for coffee.

We are caught — neither civilized nor wild.
Even in the deep forest the houses in town call us,
the families, the phone messages, the bills to be paid,
the laundry; our guilt is alive and waiting.

Out in the center of the riverbed a single boulder,
embedded in a pebble shoal, sun-washed, gleams.

Decamping, July 4

The mountains turn dark with driven clouds.
Even under the trees the staccato drops
sound like bullets on the tent all night. Our boots
are soggy with mud, clothes damp, and the air,
for all its piney tang, is thick with chill.

A nail has let the air out of our tire. We are not
Lewis and Clark. Despondent, we pile everything
into the van for the drive home on the spare,
ambivalent about our failure at rigor. West of
the Cascades the day is carelessly blue,

the garden back in town glowing in summer heat.
That night the green camp pillowcase is still on my pillow.
From bed I watch fireworks around our lake
sprinkle the dark with momentary stars. I sleep,
pretending, still, to be tented under the sighing firs.

Jordan in the Cascades

The Nooksack River splits the earth in half,
streaming down the valley like a wild mare's-tail,
carrying with it the wrecks of old trees once

livid with green. I know of a river that splinters
earth from heaven. Through my ankle bones I feel
its rough rush, its chill, its rocky bottom,

the separation, You on the other side. Here,
a liquid finger forks to a dark backwater,
a still pool of the unknown. Bending to it, I can see

only the ghost of my own face, until
the shadow of your hand lunges out of the silver,
reaching for me. Reaching for me.

Singing bowl

*The Nooksack Cirque lies in the lap of Mount Shuksan
and Mount Baker in the Cascade Mountains of Washington.*

After we have doused the light,
a few howls, then the dog settles uneasily
to sleep.

        Conversation dwindles
until there is no sound but a rattle
of dry wind against scree, like the stroking
of an animal pelt. At the foot of the cirque,
where the ice of ages melts down into
the forked river called Nooksack, we are held
in the palm of a great hand. Through the tent flap
the stars overhead radiate from
the "hammered dome," what the ancients
called the firmament, so pliant we want
to finger it, to pull it on, like a cap
against frost.

        In its wide circle beyond
the tent floor the moraine begins its curve up —
a ring of mineral difficulty rising to

the glacier's shoulders, spun with rock. Caught
in this bowl, our hearts remind us of the way
grains of sand are whirled by wind and water
within concavities in the rock face
so that, eons later, the sandstone honeycombs
into a marvel of abstract art.

                  We listen for
that rotary singing — the circular voice of the soul
ringing in our own souls, shaping us.
The chime of our creation doubles back, a hum
of matter, a gong of a word spoken
before our birth, before the golden bowl
was broken, the silver cord snapped.

                  The dog
begins again to chant his own song, pitched
to the moon rising like an orange over Shuksan.

Making a Path:
Tuolumne Meadows

Take the first step towards where
you want to go, then keep going, brushing
through the manzanitas, crushing the sweet grass
of the valley floor so its pungency
seasons the air, flowing lively as the trout stream
at your right hand, all color and gleam.
On meadow grass you are sketching a new course
that will echo the current, will skip and dodge

in and out of willow shadows on the bank
of this ancient water-path for fish. You
are no fly fisherman, but after you
the quiet carriers of rod and creel
will follow, several in a month,
and almost without thinking obey
your rabbit track, verifying the faint hollow
being carved between tufts of brittle sedge,

a coarse growth, bleached as the hair
of your children's heads in August, years ago.
Your walking has woven, unhurried
as a Kashmiri rug, a narrow runner of turf

with tufts of tan, burnt ambers, greens
fading to umber, straw. Will the winter snow
bleach out all the subtleties, and iron flat
the fabric of the field? Does this all have to be

done over every spring? How many footfalls
go to make a meadow path? Buechner said beat
a trail to God long enough, he will come to you
on the trail you have tramped, bringing you the gift
of himself. Abruptly, evening begins to shadow
the valley, but you keep pacing along and along
your own slow track. In whose fisherman boots
will you meet him, coming the other way?

Stream of consciousness

Those trips with rod and reel never send you home
empty; no poem ends at the bottom of a page.

My own darting bait of a dream floats
through your watery surface — the quick membrane

of your eye — beyond the rounded bank
of your skull, and feels its way along

a million neurons, waving like water weeds,
to a secure pool where it rests, waiting,

a sliver in your slow flow. Without fail,
almost without volition, you will catch

your own golden carp on the silver hook I
am trailing through your cerebral current.

Traveling at Home

Often my living seems to condense
from sightings into words. I've trapped
most of my adventures on these dog-eared pages —
the frost-whiskered twigs, the crunch
of iced gravel under the tires, the snuff-
colored lenticular cloud resting like a cap
on the nearest peak, the sliding by
of steam risen from the river below,
its water mirror doubling the sky's indigo — all
are written down, plucked out of winter air,
fastened to a notebook sheet
by the black, pointed pin of ink.

Here: this is my life in my hands,
traveling the blank pages like back roads.
Though the landscapes are distant, the images
dance in my mind. Their primary colors.
Last January's morning in Montana reappears
and declares itself to me, like an old love
to whom I was engaged once, proposing again.

Dic mihi, Musa

("Speak to me, Muse")

There's this . . . someone other
than me — the Muse. (She's
whispering in my ear right now.)
Sometimes she arrives unaccountably
at midnight, or just before the party,
with a small gift — a phrase, a tall tale,
a colored shape too odd to ignore —
surprisingly welcome,
usually inconvenient.

Besides being a minor deity,
mine is curator of a museum
of quirks. Also musically gifted, with
a capacity for rapture. Truthful
most of the time — only an occasional
white lie. A benevolent deity
of green plants and running water.

Merrill said, "The Muse matures
with her poet." I can imagine mine
growing slower and wiser with me,

a slight limp, and gray
in her wild hair. Already we sometimes
dream together by the lake,
lyres in hand, lazy, listening
for new alliterations.

Am I her clone, or is she mine?
She confides that we are blood-sisters —
truth, or another white lie?
It is my fond wish that someday,
when we retire together, we can lie around
amusing each other, eating grapes,
finding the most improbable words
in the Shorter Oxford.

On the river bank,
Bibury

Why do you suddenly ask me am I happy?
I am only combing my mind, like water
searching the green weed. Under the plane
tree, in this confusion of suns, crescent

trout flip their golden spines
into the air, then straighten,
heads upstream, in the clear path of water.
I know now it is their bliss to be still

in a current. The grassy fringes between glare
and dusk teach them how a river bank
casts a shadow of rest; how fixed and tranquil
lie the dark stones at river bottom.

Writing the River

After two days' rain heavy enough to
circle the view with descending silver,
Austin Creek has grown to the size of

a metaphor — rising fast from summer,
slow over pebbles, to this rowdy
torrent. Under my window it hurls itself,

with the force of myth, over river stones,
down rapids, riddled with small fish.
All day the voice of water roars

behind my writing — all day, while I'm
making soup, stoking the woodstove
(the flames rushing their orange rivers

up the flue). Under a darkened sky
I step out on the porch to check its
scouring race, and is it rising still? I know

it is myself I am checking, keeping
the window open all night to that naked,
splendid sound, dusky as pewter. Rainfall

and river together — rinsing the room,
soaking my dreams. In one dream
I am a salmon working my way up

the valley, grazed by rocks. I am living
a creek, writing a river. Downstream,
a trace of my blood feeds the lake.

Faith

Spring is a promise
in the closed fist of a long winter. All
we have got is a raw slant of light at a low
angle, a rising river of wind, and an icy rain
that drowns the green in a tide of mud. It is
the daily postponement that disillusions.
(Once more the performance has been canceled
by the management.) We live on legends
of old springs. Each evening brings
some remote possibilities of renewal:
"Maybe tomorrow?" But the evening and the
morning are the umpteenth day, and the God
of sunlit Eden still looks on the weather
and calls it — *good*.

Cosmos

"Oh now release
And let her out into the seamless world . . ."

"The Magician and the Dryad,"
C.S. Lewis

The crust is seamless. Though it shows
its scheme of cracks and geographic tracings, though
it trembles often from within or crumbles at its edges
as streams and oceans wear at it,
yet no man's ruthless stitching of a border,
no careless change of politics can wall
this earth from that, save shallowly. Fences rust.
Surveyors die. Markings fade on the maps.
Montague falls in love with Capulet. Rains
fall on us all alike in autumn and in spring,
washing away the lines. The grass roots cross
and kiss under the hedgerows, telling us
we are kin.

Subliminal messages

The telephone is silent; God doesn't return
    my calls to the office.
We're supposed to be married, but I think
    he's left me, gone
on a long trip to the Antarctic — somewhere
    cold.
The pleading letters I write him pile up,
    unsent, on the hall table;
I have no forwarding address for declarations
    of desire, invitations
To come back to me, flowers, a new book,
    a birthday present in December.
Living in the dumbness of a dead phone,
an empty mailbox,
Always, when I get home from work, the house
    is dark, the dog bored,
The plants browning, the sink piled
    with my own dirty dishes.

But yesterday the sun came out for half an hour,
whitening the curtains
From outside. Maybe it was
a message, subliminal,

Like the Two-Part Inventions
on the car radio
With Bach's questions and answers — two voices
in conversation.
Or the way the wind strokes the roof
at night
Or the rain tracks down the window glass,
intimate as tears.

Beachcombing

Suddenly, an awareness: I know, without
knowing how, that in the next minute I'll see

an aqua glint in the sand; the sea glass
sets my agenda. Or a flawless, oval pebble

shining wet at the lip of the tide rising.
Or a volute, its helix unfolding so perfectly

it must have been meant. Maybe a knot
of wood so cleanly itself, so tight in its bleached

whorl of grain, that it is hard to imagine it as
once being part of a tree. It might be

a rock that has held its secret fossil
one hundred thousand years for this moment,

its constant signal subliminal, a tone
humming along time to a tingle in my skull,

a premonition of its sly ambush in
the next few yards; the runnel

of my desire marrying the grace of God
in a current so resolute it had to happen.

Glass Beach

Mendocino, California coast, January 1997

Yesterday the gift-store clerk
told us how far up the coast
to drive: "Once it was the city dump,"
she said. The surprise
when we got there — not just
the usual glints from a polished,
occasional shard, but a whole beach
of sea glass.

Today the entire shore glitters
in the fresh light. Small, muscular ripples
rearrange the glisten of particles, hiss to the sun
here, look at this. Every wave, a quick,
inquisitive hand, turns over a new handful of
jewel pebbles for us — probing
for the rare, winking eye of cobalt,
the perfect lozenge of aqua, or bottle green,
frosted by the rub of rock, translucent
as the sea-water just now rinsing it again,
and again.

All the old discards
long gone — metals rusted away, paper, wood
shredded to nothing. Only
this shattered, sea-smoothed glass,
solid enough to survive the breakers
and turn to sapphires in our fingers.

Conch

Its open mouth corresponds
to your own hunger to hear.
Rough as the bleat
of gulls, its edges
rasp your cheek, cold as salt;
the surge of sound floods
into your own convoluted
shell of an ear
through tympanum, stapes, cochlea.

You lean into the roar — a tide
of air and water trapped
at the shell's pink, helical heart —
an ocean tumbled over
and over. Breath still moves
on the face of the deep;
you ache to its
tempest at your cheekbone.
And the inside tremor — the thunder,
the wave that breaks over
more than your bare feet.

Listen deep until it owns you.
Know the whole world
a shell, and you the grit
caught in it, being pearled over.

The singularity of shells

A shell — how small an empty space,
a folding out of pink and white,
a letting in of spiral light.
How random? And how commonplace?
(A million shells along the beach
are just as fine and full of grace
as this one here within your reach.)

But lift it, hold it to your ear
and listen. Surely you can hear
the swish and sigh of all the gray
and gleaming waters, and the play
of wind with rain and sun, encased
in one small jewel box and placed,
by God and oceans, in your way.

Polishing the
Petoskey Stone

Petoskey Stone (Hexagonaria) — a petrified colony coral
350 million years old, found on beaches in Michigan

My friend says, "Spit on it, and rub
the surface. See the pattern?"
In its hammock of lines I lift the pebble
the color of a rain cloud, cradle it
a thousand miles. Holding

the steering wheel in one hand, the gray
oval curved to my other palm, we move,
a ripple across the map to Kansas, while
I rub its softness in ellipses
against a rough shore of denim and wool.

The second day it starts
to shine like glycerin soap. As I buff it
smooth, the print rises to the surface —
the silk stone honeycombed with
eyes opening from a long sleep

between lashes of fine spines. Born
eons ago in a warm sea over
Michigan, buried in a long, restless
dream, now the old coral wakes
to the waves of cloth.

Flathead Lake, Montana

"Christ plays in ten thousand places."

Gerard Manley Hopkins

Lying here on the short grass, I am
a bowl for sunlight.

Silence. A bee. The lip lip of water
over stones. The swish and slap, hollow

under the dock. Down-shore
a man sawing wood.

Christ in the sunshine laughing
through the green translucent wings

of maple seeds. A bird
resting its song on two notes.

Rearview mirror

Cruising along at 70.
The silver oblong near your head
looks back along the highway,
your fast-receding history shining
in miniature under the cloud umbrella;
your youth a shimmer on the far horizon
of remembering; the young adult
you used to be
a pale range of distant hills.

The faint edge where earth meets sky
blurs as speed, nightfall, distance
turn you into a fleck in a landscape.
Showers take over;
even the past moment disappears
behind your car with a bend
in the road, a descent to an enigmatic valley
in the cleavage between the breasts
of hills. Ahead, the view is occluded
by evening rain. Only with an instant's glance
through the wet windshield can you see
your present place in the landscape,
this flashing moment, this ongoing now.

Amazed by love

The kinship of woman with man, of water
with stone, is a mystery — the biting of rocks
into the river's body — the lotion of water like silk
on the rough granite — a touch tender and feral,
like the wind combing a green field of oats.

A storm — all the earth trembles, and then it is still.
This astonishment, with its sudden thunder,
will shake the breath in your body the way oil
and water shiver together, and when they settle —
a strange new thing, with its pearly light.

To enter the breadth in the joining of two
is to be dazzled — there is so much space in it —
such endless possibility makes you feel smaller than
the ants on a petal, and as wide and rich
as heaven at noon. And the ocean wrapping the world

in its sapphire scarf — at water's edge, right
at your feet, you will see stones you have
never seen and never will again.
To be amazed by love is not to be blinded but
to let the flare of wonder fill you

like air filling a sail. Isn't this
the voice of God at work? Even his silence
breathes life into you, a golden sigh as fresh
as Eden. To love someone is not to lose anything,
but to gain it in giving it all away.

Found this morning

Lummi Island, January 4, 2003

Found this morning scattered across
our pebbled beach, with angled inclusions,
like white quartz lightning, slashing
across each rounded granite shape, now
I take them one by one from the heavy pack
we've carried home and spill them
onto paper, a fresh, white beach.

With what deliberate care I array them,
end to end to end, aligning the chalky stripes
so that what looks like a white string
connects them all together! Placed
so that the bright lines join, the stones
snake an arc across this wave-less shore.

What greater happiness could anyone know
than collecting accidental stones to place
end to end to end? The thing was all
tides and fortuitous circumstance, the day's
caprice (our anniversary). Intention
connecting the inadvertent. A folly,

and a confirmation of the possibilities
of linkage — eye to hand in search
and discovery, stone matching stone
in a lapidary chain, chance encounters as friend
finds friend, woman joined with man,
their eyes meeting for the first time.

acknowledgments

Grateful acknowledgment is made to the editors of the following publications, in which some of these poems first appeared:

Books & Culture: "The Golden Ratio & the Coriolis Force"

The Christian Century: "Silk," "Negligible," "Bee"

Perspectives: "Bluff Edge, Whidbey Island"

Radix: "Look!"

The poems "Freezing rain," "North St. Vrain Creek," "Vacation video," "Orienting," "Mixed media," "Edges of Wales," "The amphibian," "Seeing the Shore," "Beach, Aberystwyth, Wales," "Postcard from the shore," "Under the snowing," "Slow Passage — Teel's Island," "Faith," "Cosmos," "Subliminal messages," "Conch," "Polishing the Petoskey Stone," and "The singularity of shells" were published in *Polishing the Petoskey Stone* (Shaw, 1990).

The poems "Camping in the Rockies," "Great Blue Heron," "Trace," "Evaporation," "Labor," "Sailing San Francisco Bay," "Beach at Orient," "Spring, St. Martin's Chapel," "Making a Path: Tuolumne Meadows," "Traveling at Home," "On the river bank, Bibury," and "Writing the River" were published in *Writing the River* (Piñon Press, 1994; revised edition by Regent College Publishing, 1998).

The poems "Upon arrival from the West Coast to be with friends," "Resurrection: Rocky York Islet, B.C.," "Puzzle: Tuolumne River," "Beachcombing," "Glass Beach," and "Flathead Lake, Montana" were published in *The Angles of Light* (Shaw/Waterbook, 2000; used by permission of the publisher).